# INCREDIBLE MOMENTS WITH THE SAVIOR

## *Learning to see*

KEN GIRE

Daybreak Books

Zondervan Publishing House
Grand Rapids, Michigan

Incredible Moments with the Savior
Copyright © 1990 by Ken Gire

Daybreak Books are published by
the Zondervan Publishing House
1415 Lake Drive, S.E.
Grand Rapids, Michigan 49506

**Library of Congress Cataloging-in-Publication Data**

Gire, Ken
    Incredible moments with the Savior / Ken Gire.
      p. cm.
    ISBN 0-310-21790-3
    1. Jesus Christ—Miracles—Meditations. 2. Bible. N.T. Gospels—
    Meditations. I. Title.
    BT366.G57 1990
    232.9'5—dc20                                            90-31281
                                                              CIP

Published in association with the literary agency of Sealy M. Yates and
associates, Orange, California.

*Printed in the United States of America*

90  91  92  93  94 / DH / 10  9  8  7  6  5  4  3  2

This edition is printed on acid-free paper and meets the American
National Standards Institute Z39.48 standard.

edicated to

Jack and Hertha Herweg

For entrusting me with
your daughter and grandchildren
as I embarked on a career as uncertain and unstable
as that of a writer.
I hope when I have a son-in-law someday,
that I will show him as much kindness and respect
as you have shown to me.

# CONTENTS

*"We have seen his glory,*

*the glory of the One and Only,*

*who came from the Father,*

*full of grace and truth."*

# INTRODUCTION

n the daily routine of private devotions and in the weekly ritual of worship, the incredible moments in our Savior's life often become shopworn and lose much of their luster.

When that happens, those moments cease to be sacred ground. Consequently, we no longer take off our shoes and fall on our faces before them. Why? Because wonder is prerequisite to worship, and when we lose our sense of wonder, we lose the dynamic that brings us to our knees.

Our Lord's life was replete with incredible moments. Everywhere he went people's breaths were taken away by what he did. Their mouths fell open in amazement. Their faces paled in fear. And from village to village the comments were the same: "We have never seen anything like this before."

The purpose of this book is to restore some of the wonder that has been lost over the years so that Jesus can been seen in all his splendor.

Learning to see Jesus. That's what this book is all about. To do that I have focused on the precise moments when his glory was revealed—moments when the veil of his humanity was lifted to let his deity shine forth. Merciful moments like the healing of the leper. Dramatic moments like the calming of the storm. Tearful moments like the raising of Lazarus.

These incredible moments filled the people who saw them with awe, and their lives were never the same. Some came into the light. Others tried to extinguish it. But all their lives bore the imprint of those fleeting flashes of glory.

This book is merely a rustic attempt to put frames around a few of those flashes of glory.

I hope that the pictures fill your heart with wonder for our truly incredible Savior. And I hope that heart becomes so full it overflows with compassion for those who hurt—for they were the ones on whom his glory was so freely poured out.

Ken Gire

# AN
# INCREDIBLE MOMENT
## AT A
## WEDDING

⌁

# SCRIPTURE

n the third day a wedding took place at Cana in Galilee. Jesus' mother was there, and Jesus and his disciples had been invited to the wedding. When the wine was gone, Jesus' mother said to him, "They have no more wine."

"Dear woman, why do you involve me?" Jesus replied, "My time has not yet come."

His mother said to the servants, "Do whatever he tells you."

Nearby stood six stone water jars, the kind used by the Jews for ceremonial washing, each holding from twenty to thirty gallons.

Jesus said to the servants, "Fill the jars with water"; so they filled them to the brim.

Then he told them, "Now draw some out and take it to the master of the banquet."

They did so, and the master of the banquet tasted the water that had been turned into wine. He did not realize where it had come from, though the servants who had drawn the water knew. Then he called the bridegroom aside and said, "Everyone brings out the choice wine first and then the cheaper wine after the guests have had too much to drink; but you have saved the best till now."

This, the first of his miraculous signs, Jesus performed in Cana of Galilee. He thus revealed his glory, and his disciples put their faith in him.

*John 2:1–11*

# MEDITATION

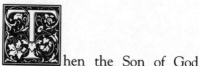hen the Son of God
stepped down from his throne to become a man, the finest
of heaven's wines funneled itself into the common earthen
vessel of a Palestinian Jew.

For thirty years this vintage from heaven was cellared
away in a carpenter's shop in Nazareth. But now the time
has come for the seal to be broken, the cork extracted,
and the fragrant bouquet of deity to fill the earth so that,
for a fleeting but festive moment, the world's parched lips
might taste the kingdom of God.

That time coincides, appropriately, with a wedding.

For the overworked, the underpaid, and the punitively
taxed, the wedding was a much needed reprieve when they
could relax with old friends and together share a little
food, a little wine, a little laughter.

But the laughter was beginning to wane. The poor
family hosting the wedding had hoped the wine could be
stretched by watering down what they had and by filling
the goblets only half full. But now they were down to dregs
at the bottom of the wine jars.

In an effort to spare the family any embarrassment or
social disgrace, Jesus' mother comes to him for help.
Wringing her hands, she states anxiously, "They have no
more wine." Her implication is "Do something."

Since Jesus' miraculous birth, Mary has pondered in
her heart the future glory of her son. She has seen the
visions, heard the angels, and witnessed his remarkable
development. Now as she implores her son, she expects

3

him to rise to the occasion of need and pour out something of his glory to fill that need.

There is a moment of hesitation after the impassioned plea. During that brief moment Mary looks into her son's face and sees a decidedly different man than the one who has lived with her and cared for her the last thirty years. His face bears the chiseled sculpting from his forty days in the wilderness. He is leaner now, more serious, more intense.

Jesus hesitates because he knows that if he meets this need by supernatural means, life will never be the same. Never again could he turn back the clock.

No, after this one wedding, the small-town seclusion of his life would be forever behind him. For the next three and a half years, his only time to himself would be stolen moments in an olive grove before dawn or snatches of quiet on a barren knoll after dark. Fellowship with his Father would then come only at the expense of sleep, so great were the needs of the people who would press about him during the day in so many cities, on so many hillsides, and by so many seashores.

Everywhere he would go, Jesus would become the embroidered gossip of women and the anvil of debate among men. With scribal precision every jot and tittle of Jesus' teaching would be tested against the touchstone of rabbinic tradition. Everywhere he would go, communities would bob in his wake, sending unsettling ripples throughout Palestine.

Understandably, as he weighs the alternatives, Jesus

holds the request at bay.

"Dear woman, why do you involve me? My time has not yet come."

In the hidden arena where his mind wrestles with the request, Jesus feels the grip of yet another consideration—it is too soon to reveal his glory. All the disciples have not yet been chosen. Many of the plans for his ministry are still just pencil sketches in his mind, awaiting color and dimension from the hand of the Father.

The Father. Jesus would hesitate again at a future request. "Father, if you are willing, take this cup from me." The fateful cup would be difficult to take. The brimming wrath would be hard to swallow. But with a trembling hand Jesus *would* take that cup. "Yet not my will, but yours be done."

And so, just as he would submit to his Father's request at Gethsemane, he would submit now to his mother's request at Cana.

His thoughts turn quickly from the future to the need of the moment. To the people, so poor and so heavily burdened. To those shackled to a life of drudgery, so in want of a little festive pleasure in their lives. To the parents of the bride and groom, so frazzled with all their preparations, so indebted to provide this wedding.

At last his thoughts turn to the bride and groom. The embarrassment would be no way to start a honeymoon, let alone a new home in the community. The young couple needed help. And his heart went out to them.

❧

Without a word from his lips, without a touch from his hand, Jesus simply wills the water to become wine. And in the sacred presence of that thought, the water prostrates itself and obeys.

So characteristic of the Savior that he would first reveal his glory *here,* in *this* way, and for *this* purpose.

It was not revealed at the imperial palace in Rome. Or at Herod's temple in Jerusalem. Or at the colonnaded Acropolis in Athens. But *here,* in an impoverished village of Cana, nestled away in an obscure corner of Galilee.

And the *way* he revealed his glory—with a quiet miracle. No fanfare. No footlights. No theatrics. Just the mighty hand of God working silently behind the scenes in an hour of need.

And the *purpose* of the miracle—performed not to quench his own thirst, but to satisfy the needs of others. To ease a dear woman's anxiety. To save a couple of starry-eyed newlyweds from embarrassment. And to provide a little pleasure for a work-worn community.

The unveiled glory enlarged the disciples' faith. And it did one other thing. With that decision to reveal his glory, Jesus crossed the Rubicon—that river of no return.

The die was cast.

The clock was wound. It would begin ticking down to the final hour of his destiny and set in motion the gears that would ultimately enmesh him and cost him his life. For the wine he provided at Cana would hasten the cup he would one day drink at the cross.

❦

# PRAYER

ear Lord Jesus,

Truly, heaven saves the best wine until last. So different from the way the world ladles out its pleasures. First there is the giddy exhilaration, but with the morning comes the headache and the heartache. And that's when the gnawing emptiness returns.

Lord, someone close to my heart has gone through life with that gnawing emptiness, aching for something more.

I pray that you would take _____ and fill him with your Spirit. His heart, with its dry hollow contours, yearns for you, but he doesn't know it. His soul is too unschooled in spiritual things to even articulate the ache.

He has sought to satisfy that ache with all the wrong things, Lord. But he is an empty man, whose past is filled with regret, whose present is filled with distractions, and whose future is filled with worry.

Empty him of these, Lord. Even if you have to turn his life upside down to do it.

Fill him with the brimming awareness that you—who are the same yesterday, today, and forever—that you forgive his past, that you are his soul's daily bread, and that you hold his future in your hands.

I'm trusting you for a miracle, Lord. Touch the water of his life and transform it into the finest of wines. . . .

# AN
## INCREDIBLE MOMENT
## WITH A
## ROYAL OFFICIAL

❥

# SCRIPTURE

nce more he visited Cana in Galilee, where he had turned the water into wine. And there was a certain royal official whose son lay sick at Capernaum. When this man heard that Jesus had arrived in Galilee from Judea, he went to him and begged him to come and heal his son, who was close to death.

"Unless you people see miraculous signs and wonders," Jesus told him, "you will never believe."

The royal official said, "Sir, come down before my child dies."

Jesus replied, "You may go. Your son will live."

The man took Jesus at his word and departed. While he was still on the way, his servants met him with the news that his boy was living. When he inquired as to the time when his son got better, they said to him, "The fever left him yesterday at the seventh hour."

Then the father realized that this was the exact time at which Jesus had said to him, "Your son will live." So he and all his household believed.

*John 4:46–53*

# MEDITATION

he word translated "royal official" literally means *king's man*. He is one of Herod's most trusted officials. He resides in the town of Capernaum, probably in a well-manicured villa on a chalky cliff overlooking the scalloped blue sparkle of the Galilean Sea. His is a soft-cushioned life with servants padding around the estate to attend to his every need.

He has wealth and rank and privilege. But none of these can help him now. Not even Herod, with all his imperial jurisdiction, can help.

A high temperature has reduced his little boy of boundless energy to a limp rag doll, melting feverishly away into the bedsheets.

The man's service to Herod has rewarded him well. A beautiful home. A tableau of ornate furnishings. Epicurean delights to satiate the most discriminating of palates. Clothes suitable for the king's most elaborate fetes. He is a wealthy man. Understandably, when his son fell sick, his wealth was the first thing he turned to.

He hired the best physicians money could buy. But a clutter of vials by the boy's bedside gives mute testimony to their agnostic diagnoses.

The father has exhausted everything from exotic medicines prescribed by professionals to folk remedies suggested by his servants. He would try anything now. He's desperate. The delight of his life is slipping away before his very eyes.

He and his wife stay up all night hovering over the boy, sponging down his inflamed body. Servants shuffle in and out to change the sheets, to bring dry towels and fresh basins of water and a few words of consolation.

But now, there is nothing more that can be done. Except to wait. And hope.

Sadly, the Galilean dawn fails to send even a pale ray of hope their way. The official sits on the terrace, staring blankly at the impassive sea. His eyes are puffy from the night-long vigil; his body, numb; his heart, a dull ache.

And pulsing from that heart is a relentless rhythm of questions: What would all the trappings of success matter if he loses his boy? What would his job matter? Or his rambling estate? Or anything?

In an incriminating moment of truth he realizes that all his wealth, all his rank, all his privilege mean nothing. He would gladly trade them for the life of his son. But that is one thing his money can't buy.

The painful throb of questions continues.

What would it be like without his son playing in the yard, building his little pretend fortresses among the rose trellises? What would it be like without him scampering through the house, his boyish noises trailing playfully in his wake? What would it be like not setting a place for him at the dinner table?

The father buries his face in his hands and weeps for his son—the little boy he may never again tuck into bed . . . the playworn little legs he may never again rub . . . the eager little ears he may never again tell bedtime stories to.

❧

*Never again.* The thought falls on him with the sharp finality of an executioner's blade.

His royal, official palms are wet with regret. For working too hard. For being gone too much. For missing out on so many of the priceless moments in his little boy's childhood. Moments he could never buy back, regardless of his wealth, rank, or privilege.

He sits slumped in a despondent heap.

When the day servants begin their shift, one of them ventures hesitantly to his side to tell him about Jesus— about the incredible things people were saying about him . . . about this miraculous power he had to heal the sick . . . and maybe, maybe if he could just talk Jesus into coming to see the boy . . .

No sooner is the suggestion proffered than the official readies himself for the twenty-five mile trek to Cana, where Jesus is staying.

He arrives at the village in a frenetic search for this miracle worker, for Jesus is his last hope.

Finding him, he does something uncharacteristic for a man of his position—he begs. He begs for the life of his little boy—the little boy he will never hug again, never see grow up, if Jesus doesn't come to his bedside.

Oddly, Jesus doesn't respond with the compassion that is so characteristic of him. Instead, he rebukes the man.

"Unless you people see miraculous signs and wonders, you will never believe."

Jesus had been front-page news in Palestine. But the news making the rounds was sensationalistic. And the atmosphere surrounding Christ was fast becoming that of a circus—"Step right up and see signs and wonders performed before your very eyes! Come one, come all! See the Miracle Worker in action!"

That's not what Jesus wanted. He didn't want to become a side-show attraction. He didn't want the kingdom of God to become some cotton candy experience that would melt sweetly in their mouths and then be gone.

With his hands clutching Jesus' robe, the royal official falls to his knees, pleading, begging, imploring.

"Sir, come down before my child dies."

His voice cracks as tears wend their way down his cheeks. The spilling emotion flashes a memory in Jesus' mind. He remembers *his* father's eyes, the paternal concern in them, the love, the emotion. He knows he will see those same eyes again when he goes to heaven, but suddenly, the chronic ache of not seeing his father becomes acute. He remembers the painful rending of their last embrace. He turns his eyes to the man on his knees.

"You may go. Your son will live."

For a moment the father hesitates. The answer is not quite what he expected. He expected Jesus to return with him. But as the father rises from his knees, he takes a step of faith. He takes Jesus at his word and turns his tear-streaked face toward home.

A seed has been sown in the tear-soaked soil of that

father's heart. And with the decision to take Jesus at his word, the first stirrings of faith begin to germinate.

The man would be up early the next morning. He would return home to the embrace of his servants, his wife . . . and his little boy.

Faith would spring to life and take root in that garden villa overlooking the sea. And there it would flourish, its scented blossoms cascading over the terraced walls, bursting with iridescent colors.

Colors this father had never seen before. Colors so vibrant that all his wealth, all his rank, all his privilege paled by comparison. Colors that highlighted to this prominent man what was really important in life—the son he now held in his arms . . . and the Savior he now held in his heart.

# PRAYER

ear Beloved Son
of the Father,

Thank you for the beauty and the fragrance and the color you have given to my life. As the flower bends toward the sun, may I seek you every waking hour.

Help me to seek you with the fervency of that royal official, but help me to seek you with the same fervency when all is well as when all is not well.

I confess that the comforts of this world so often insulate me from the reality of how much I need you. Help me see that the hard mercies of adversity are not stones thrown to hurt me but stones that serve to get my attention —to tap on the window of my comfortable estate and remind me that this is not my home.

Grant me the grace to take those hard mercies, no matter how sharp or how heavy, and use them to pave a road to you. Help me to see that those same stones form the wide road over which your tender mercies make their way to me.

Lord Jesus, tear off the blinders that fix my eyes only on my narrow, little path of pain. Lift my head to see the hard roads others have to travel.

For those others I now pray, O Lord. For those who are losing a loved one, I pray you would bring clarity to their circumstances and comfort to their careworn hearts. For those who have lost a loved one, I pray you would take them in your arms and hold them.

Especially I pray for _____ and _____ who suffer

the special hurt of a child that is seriously ill. This is a hard mercy for them, Lord. Grant them the grace to use that stone to pave a path to your feet. And there, I pray, grant them the same tender mercy you gave to that royal official, the assurance that their child will live. Please. . . .

# AN
# INCREDIBLE MOMENT
# WITH A
# PARALYTIC

❧

# SCRIPTURE

 few days later, when Jesus again entered Capernaum, the people heard that he had come home. So many gathered that there was no room left, not even outside the door, and he preached the word to them. Some men came, bringing to him a paralytic, carried by four of them. Since they could not get him to Jesus because of the crowd, they made an opening in the roof above Jesus and, after digging through it, lowered the mat the paralyzed man was lying on. When Jesus saw their faith, he said to the paralytic, "Son, your sins are forgiven."

Now some teachers of the law were sitting there, thinking to themselves, "Why does this fellow talk like this? He's blaspheming! Who can forgive sins but God alone?"

Immediately Jesus knew in his spirit that this was what they were thinking in their hearts, and he said to them, "Why are you thinking these things? Which is easier: to say to the paralytic, 'Your sins are forgiven,' or to say, 'Get up, take your mat and walk?' But that you may know that the Son of Man has authority on earth to forgive sins. . . ." He said to the paralytic, "I tell you, get up, take your mat and go home." He got up, took his mat and walked out in full view of them all. This amazed everyone and they praised God, saying, "We have never seen anything like this!"

*Mark 2:1–12*

# MEDITATION

s a paralytic he stares a
bleak future in the face. For there were no neurosurgeons
back then, no specialists, no convalescent hospitals, no
physical therapists, no medical breakthroughs on the horizon, no miracle drugs in the medicine cabinet.

Sympathy is the only prescription the community could
dispense. And he's had enough of that. He doesn't want
sympathy. He wants his life back.

The life he has now is a horizontal one, full of bedsores
and blank stares at the ceiling. It is his only priest, that
ceiling. But it neither acknowledges his confessions nor
accepts his penance.

His spindly legs and arms form the bars to the cell that
imprisons him, isolating him from the rest of the world.
And so there he lays, alone on a 3x6 mat. Day after day.
Week after week. Month after monotonous month.

Never able to rise and stretch with the morning sun.
Never able to socialize in the streets. Never able to step
out for a casual breath of fresh air. Never able to walk off
his frustrations. Never able to have a change of scenery
without inconveniencing a handful of other people.

He has to rely on others for everything. For every sip
of water. For every bite of food. For every time his bowels
moved or his bladder needed relief. Somebody else has to
turn him, and bathe him, and clothe him.

Dependency. Humiliation. Confinement. Boredom.
Loneliness. Frustration. Shame. Despair. These are just
a few of the entries in the thesaurus that defines life
on a 3x6 mat.

But for all the pejorative synonyms, this paralytic has one positive word that gives his life a syllable of meaning: *friends*. Four faithful friends. And these friends have heard some incredible things that bring them to his bedside. They come with exciting news of a miracle worker.

Ever since Jesus exorcised a demon from a man in the synagogue, news crested out from Capernaum in waves. It lapped the shore cities on the Sea of Galilee. It rippled throughout the Decapolis. And it washed up as far south as Jerusalem.

When a second wave of news went out about the healing of a leper, the crowds swelled. People flooded into Capernaum from everywhere. They came to see this phenomenon called *the Nazarene*.

They were a catch-all collection of seekers, spectators, and spies. Some came with a hopeful eye, to be healed. Others came with a curious eye, to be convinced. Still others came with a jaundiced eye. To find out who was rocking the religious boat and to stop him from making any more waves.

The house where Jesus is speaking today is packed. Late-comers are wedged into the entrance, standing on tiptoes, cupping their ears to catch a few of the teacher's words.

One of the late-comers is the paralytic, carried by his four friends, each shouldering a corner of the mat. But the wall of flesh proves impenetrable. And with their repeated attempts they are shushed and waved away by the impatient crowd straining to hear.

~

Not to be denied, the determined men back off and brainstorm another approach. "The stairs. What about the outside stairs to the roof?"

Their enthusiasm mounts with every step they ascend. When they reach the top, their hearts are pounding in their throats. Laying their friend down, they survey the roof to pinpoint where Jesus is standing. Then, with adrenalin pumping, they remove the clay tiles and begin burrowing.

The falling debris creates a billowy cloud of dust and sends the crowd scooting back, coughing their complaints into their hands.

Their eyes angle upward, and the first thing they see is a tangle of fingers worming their way to widen the hole. They see a shaft of sunlight, a pair of eyes searching for Jesus, then four pairs of hands widening the hole, and finally, the bottom of the paralytic's mat.

The friends strain to lower the paralyzed man as several men below stretch to ease the mat to the floor.

From the opening in the roof spills an inverted funnel of light, where flecks of dust pirouette in an evanescent ballet, dancing spritely around the limp man on the floor.

Jesus' eyes are transfixed on the four heads circling the hole in the ceiling. The text says he "saw their faith." *Their* faith. The faith of the paralytic's friends. It is on the wings of their faith that the mercy from heaven descends.

There's no record that they said anything. So it wasn't what Jesus *heard* that captured his heart; it was what he *saw*.

ᕷ

And what did he see? Four, sweaty men willing to put a shoulder to their faith . . . scraped hands willing to burrow through any obstacles . . . dirty faces, hungering for a miracle. Breathless with excitement. Wide-eyed with anticipation. Like street children pressing their noses against a bakery window, they were famished for a sweet taste of heaven.

These children dared what no adults with any sense of etiquette would ever have done. They tore up somebody's property, interrupted somebody else while he was speaking, and inconvenienced all the rest who were listening. Just like children.

But he who said "Suffer the children to come unto me" didn't look at these children of faith as an interruption. Quite the contrary. For these were children of his Father's household.

Jesus' gaze falls on the wrung-out dishrag of a man who lies plopped at his feet. He sees that the paralysis is deeper than it appears. Within that emaciated body lies a crippled soul, paralyzed from sin, atrophied from shame.

The man looks up, his eyelids fluttering to shield him from the sun. Jesus stands over him and eclipses the light. For a moment heaven opens. The face of God smiles. And a sweet piece of manna falls to the man on the mat.

"Son, your sins are forgiven."

How long has he waited to hear those words? How many tears has he cried to the stoic ceiling that looked down on him, pleading for an answer to the enigma of his life?

Jesus spoke with a smile as if to say, "Be of good cheer, my child, God is not angry with you." With quivering lips the paralytic smiles back. He fights back the tears, but it's no use. He squeezes his eyes shut, and years of pent-up pain spill from his eyes to stream down the sides of his face.

But the tender mercies that stroke the cheeks of the paralytic come as a slap in the face to the religious leaders. While heaven rejoices, they are too busy scribbling mental notes to join in the dance. They reason syllogistically:

> *Jesus claims the power to forgive sins.*
> *Only God can forgive sins.*
> *Therefore Jesus claims to be God.*

Precisely the point. Their reasoning was exact. It brought them to the right conclusion, but it didn't bring them to Christ. If that hole in the roof teaches us anything, it's that faith is what brings a person to Jesus, not intellectual reasonings. Curiosity crowded the classroom, but it was faith that dug through the roof to bring the paralytic to the feet of Christ.

Jesus reads his critics' minds as if to offer further proof that he is who he claims to be.

"Why are you thinking these things? Which is easier: to say to the paralytic, 'Your sins are forgiven,' or to say, 'Get up, take your mat and walk?' But that you may know that the Son of Man has authority on earth to forgive sins . . . ."

Both are equally easy *to say.* But both are equally impossible *to do.* Unless, of course, you're God. In that case one is as easy as the other, which explains Jesus' nonchalance. But so the religious leaders won't write him off as just a faith healer, Jesus does what no mere mortal would be presumptuous enough to do—he forgives the man his sins against God.

The Savior puts a final punctuation point on the debate and turns his attention from the skeptics to the paralytic.

"Take up your mat and go home."

Even with the paralysis healed, the atrophied muscles would have made the man wobble like a newborn colt. But the paralytic receives grace upon grace. Not only is he given forgiveness and healing, he is given back his strength.

Getting up, he heaves his mat over his shoulder, praising God all the way out the door. And the crowd that refused him entrance reverently parts to make way for his exit.

There is a mingling of awe, amazement, and fear. "We have never seen anything like this."

It was a bright, shining moment for the kingdom of God and an incredible moment for the people in that room. For through the hole in that low roof came the glory of a distant kingdom, glinting from the crown of its king.

Outside, dancing in the street to the glory of that king, are five friends who have the joy of heaven streaming down their cheeks. Five friends who have become children . . . all over again.

# Prayer

ear Son of Man,

Thank you for the handful of faithful friends who once carried me on their shoulders and brought me to you. Thank you that no matter how lame my excuses, they refused to leave me resigned to my pallet.

Thank you for _____ and _____ and _____ and _____. Thank you for their faith. Thank you for all the trouble they went to.

No matter how large the crowd, they were willing to find a way through. No matter how steep the stairs, they were willing to climb. No matter how thick the roof, they were willing to dig.

For all the obstacles they overcame to bring me to you, I thank you, Lord Jesus.

Thank you for how much they loved, how much they cared, how much they prayed, how much they shouldered. I will never be able to thank them enough—or you.

Thank you for giving me my life back. Thank you for making me whole. Thank you for being so understanding and so willing to forgive.

In remembrance of the grace shown to me, help me now to turn my heart to those who are bent or broken or bedridden. To those who are confined to wheelchairs or to hospital beds or to quiet, lonely rooms where the light of human friendship seldom shines.

Help me to be a friend to someone whose body is a prison, knowing that you have called me to visit the prisoners as though in prison with them, and knowing that when I have done it unto the least of these, I have done it unto you.

Help me to be sensitive to other forms of paralysis that lie *below* the surface. To those crippled by some debilitating set of circumstances. To those immobilized by some chronic disease of the soul. To those stunned by divorce. To those numbed by the death of a loved one. To those buried under a heavy load of depression. To those bearing an injury of the heart. To those shattered by a broken relationship. For any crippling influences that have devastated their lives, I pray, Lord Jesus. Help me to put a shoulder to my faith by lifting them up in prayer, by bearing their burdens, and by bringing them to you to find mercy. Especially I pray for _____. . . .

# AN
# INCREDIBLE MOMENT
# WITH A
# LEPER

☙

# SCRIPTURE

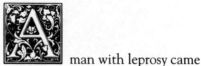 man with leprosy came to him and begged him on his knees, "If you are willing, you can make me clean."

Filled with compassion, Jesus reached out his hand and touched the man. "I am willing," he said. "Be clean!" Immediately the leprosy left him and he was cured.

Jesus sent him away at once with a strong warning: "See that you don't tell this to anyone. But go, show yourself to the priest and offer the sacrifices that Moses commanded for your cleansing, as a testimony to them." Instead he went out and began to talk freely, spreading the news. As a result, Jesus could no longer enter a town openly but stayed outside in lonely places. Yet the people still came to him from everywhere.

*Mark 1:40–45*

# MEDITATION

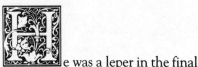e was a leper in the final
stages of decay. Luke described him as "covered with
leprosy."

It's a horrible disease, leprosy. It begins with little
specks on the eyelids and on the palms of the hand. Then
it spreads over the body. It bleaches the hair white. It
casts a cadaverous pallor over the skin, crusting it with
scales and erupting over it with oozing sores.

But that's just what happens on the surface. Penetrat-
ing the skin, the disease, like a moth, eats its way through
the weave of nerves reticulated throughout the body's
tissues. Soon the body becomes numb to the point of
sensory deprivation, numbed to both pleasure and pain.
A toe can break, and it will register no pain. And sensing
no pain, the leper will continue walking, only to worsen
the break and hasten the infection. One by one the ap-
pendages of the leper suffer their fate against the hard
edges of life.

And if the physical stigma of the disease isn't enough,
the rabbis attach a moral stigma to it as well. They believe
it to be a direct blow by God on the backs of the sinful.
And with that belief comes a rigid catechism of cause-and-
effect platitudes—"No death without sin, no pain without
transgression." For them, leprosy is a visual symbol of
moral decay. It begins with a small speck that slowly but
surely destroys the individual.

Levitical regulations require the leper's outer garment
to be torn, the hair unkempt, and the face partially covered. He dresses as a mourner going to a burial service—*his*
burial service. And he must call out to those he passes on

the way, "Unclean! Unclean!" An announcement both of his physical and of his moral death.

He must keep at least six feet away when he passes. And as he passes, he is shunned. Little children run from him. Older ones shoo him with stones and sharp-cornered remarks. Adults walk on the other side of the street, mutter a prayer for him under their breath, shake their heads in disgust, or simply look the other way.

He lives not only with the horror of the disease but also with its shame and its guilt.

There is no cure for the man. He is forced to live outside the walls of the city, shuffled off to a leper colony. There, on the far horizons of humanity, he is sentenced to live out his days. Again, another symbol. This time of his separation from God.

At the colony, food is lowered to the entrance of his cave, a cave crowded with the miserable and the hopeless. Then those who brought the food scurry away like frightened barn mice.

The leper's life is one of isolation. Like the disease, the isolation progresses gradually but completely. First his peripheral friends drop out of sight. Then his closer circle of friends constricts, shrinking smaller and smaller until, at last, he's left with only a tiny center of immediate family. And, one by one, even they stop coming by so often. Then one day he realizes his mother is the only one who comes anymore. Her visits are shorter and less frequent. And she stands farther away, without looking him in the eyes as she used to.

↓

The hollow cave he lives in is a symbol, too. A symbol of his loneliness. His is a hard life of muted grays that grow darker and darker with each day. He huddles in the cold and shadowy recesses of that cave with only occasional, faint echoes entering from the outside world.

There he lives. Without love. Without hope. Without the simple joys and dignities of life: being smiled at . . . being greeted on the street . . . buying fresh fruit in the market . . . talking politics by the public fountain . . . laughing . . . getting up to go to work . . . operating a business . . . haggling over prices with a shopkeeper . . . getting a wedding invitation . . . singing hymns in the synagogue . . . celebrating Passover with family.

All these are barred to him. Forever.

I wonder. How long has it been since someone has shaken his hand . . . patted him on the back . . . put an arm around his waist . . . rubbed his shoulders . . . hugged him . . . stroked his hair . . . touched his cheek . . . wiped a tear from his eye . . . or kissed him?

He wakes early this morning from a dream of those times, times when people loved him, touched him. But it's just a dream. Reality is the cave. And the colony.

This morning the colony is abuzz with news about Jesus being in town. Jesus, the one claiming to be the Son of God. The one who heals the sick, makes the lame walk, and opens the eyes of the blind.

The news sparks hope to this dimly burning wick. Surreptitiously he slips away. Hobbling off to find this

Jesus. And the closer he gets, the more brightly hope burns within him.

At last he arrives. But the throng of people clustered around Jesus is too intent to notice his approach. Timidly, he shuffles his way uncertainly along the frayed edge of the crowd, watching, listening. With each person Jesus heals, a wave of wonder crashes over the crowd and foams at the leper's feet.

Trembling with excitement, he dares what he would never do with a rabbi. He dares to draw near.

As he does, the crowd parts dramatically. A leper is in their midst. Some stand by silently and watch the lowly reverence of his approach. Others murmur their indignance. But no one stands in his way.

He stops within arm's distance of Jesus and falls at his feet. The man looks up and begs. His plea is halting yet direct, "If you are willing, you can make me clean."

Jesus looks at the glimmer of faith in the man's sunken eyes. He looks at the ashen skin. He sees the sores. He sees the shame.

Without beauty, without bloom, this pale, wilted flower bows before the Savior. A grim reminder of how the thorns have taken over paradise.

The sight fills Jesus with compassion. He reaches out to touch the man. Reaches out to touch a leper.

The gesture says so much to someone nobody speaks to anymore, let alone touches. It says, "I love you. I care. I'm sorry. I understand. I want to help."

And with that touch, goosebumps flutter over little pools of feeling that still remain on his skin. Jesus doesn't delay in putting an end to the man's suffering. "I am willing. Be clean."

Another surge rushes over the leper. This time he feels it all the way to his toes. He looks down at his hands. Gone is the sickly color. Gone are the sores. He tests the fingertips. There is feeling. He clenches to make a fist. There is strength.

He looks back up at Jesus. His eyes pool with emotion as he tries to speak. But it feels as though his whole sad life is lodged sideways in his throat, and the words can't get through.

Soon, the words will come. Then he will tell everyone he sees. He will tell about his cleansing. And he will tell about a wonderfully willing Savior who reached out and touched a leper.

# PRAYER

ear Jesus,

I come to you on my knees, praying on behalf of someone who sees herself as a leper. I plead for your compassion
on _____.

She is a lonely person, Lord. She stands on the peri-
phery of social circles, darting her eyes away or lowering
her head self-consciously. She's afraid of the stares of the
more secure. Afraid they will see her spots . . . her sores
. . . her shame.

If you are willing, Lord, you can make her clean.

Help her to realize that we all have sins. Some on the
surface that are evident to all. Some that are hidden deep
within. Sins that no one sees, except you. And yet when
you see the leprous abcesses of our hearts, you don't flinch
and recoil—you reach out, to touch and to heal.

She needs you, Jesus, but she is ashamed to come near,
thinking she's too unclean for your presence. Help her to
remember that it is the sick for whom you came. And help
her to come to you for healing. There may she find understanding in your eyes, acceptance in your smile, and tenderness in your touch.

If you are willing, Lord, you can make her clean.

She longs to hear from you the words that leper heard,
"I am willing. Be clean." Help her to realize that you are
not only *able* to cleanse her but that you are *willing*. Reach
out to her, Lord. Touch her. Make her whole.

Give me a heart that is filled with compassion for this
woman—the same compassion you were filled with when

you saw that leper, standing on the outskirts of humanity. Give me arms that are willing to reach out to her, Lord. And hands that aren't afraid to touch and get involved in her life. . . .

# AN
# INCREDIBLE MOMENT
# AT NAIN

# SCRIPTURE

oon afterward, Jesus went to a town called Nain, and his disciples and a large crowd went along with him. As he approached the town gate, a dead person was being carried out—the only son of his mother, and she was a widow. And a large crowd from the town was with her. When the Lord saw her, his heart went out to her and he said, "Don't cry."

Then he went up and touched the coffin, and those carrying it stood still. He said, "Young man, I say to you, get up!" The dead man sat up and began to talk, and Jesus gave him back to his mother.

They were filled with awe and praised God. "A great prophet has appeared among us," they said. "God has come to help his people." This news about Jesus spread throughout Judea and the surrounding country.

*Luke 7:11–17*

# MEDITATION

ain is a cozy community carved out of a rocky slope overlooking the valley of Jezreel. It is springtime, and the valley is a sea of wind-blown grass, frothing with wildflowers; the air, redolent with the blossoms of fruit trees.

But in the valley of this widow's heart, it is the dead of winter.

Twice, death has reached its icy fingers into her family and wrenched loved ones from her. First her husband. Now her son. Her *only* son.

For years she has faced an uncertain future. Now she faces it alone. With no one to hold her hand. With no one to steady her steps.

No one to comfort her when she cries herself to sleep at night. No one to wake up to in the morning. No one to fix breakfast for. No one to share the holy days, or the common days, or any days at all for that matter. No one to grow old with. And no one to look after her in the autumn of her life.

No one.

Nothing remains but an empty shell of a house. A house that years ago gave up waiting for a husband to come home from work. And now, no longer waits for that husband's son.

The sagging house is slumped in its own grief, retreating into itself, silent and still. There are no sounds of animated talk that chronicle the day. No ripples of laughter. No late-night conversations. Only quiet tributaries of grief running from room to room.

❦

Bundled in her heart is too-short a stack of memories. Not enough to cloak her from the chill of her present loneliness, let alone to keep her warm in her old age.

The open coffin leads the way to the cemetery outside of town. Trailing in its wake is the weeping mother, relatives, close friends, and other mourners. Interspersed throughout the procession are the melancholy, dove-like calls of flutes and the plaintive tinkling of cymbals. A chorus of women chant their laments while men pray and plod along in silent vigil.

But at the same time this crowd is leaving Nain, another crowd is entering. The one is following a coffin; the other is following Christ. The one is filled with sorrow and despair; the other, with excitement and hope.

In respect for the dead the crowd following Jesus pulls back, allowing the funeral procession to thread its way through the gate.

There, life and death stand on two distinct islands. The bridge between the two is a mother's grief, arching over a torrent of tears.

When Jesus sees the tears wrung from the mother's heart, every thought that had preoccupied him on his journey flees. The whole of his attention focuses on this shattered woman.

All he knows is her desperation. All he feels is her pain. All he sees is her tears.

And those tears are the flame that melts his heart.

Jesus extends his hand to touch the coffin, and the

procession lurches to a stop. He isn't concerned with protocol or etiquette or even with the fact that touching a coffin would render him unclean in the eyes of rabbinic law. His only concern is for this despondent mother.

"Don't cry."

The words are not out of a textbook on pastoral care. They seep from the cracks of a heart bursting with compassion. Jesus turns to the woman's son.

"Young man, I say to you, get up."

Two words to the bereaved, eight to the deceased. But that is enough. Enough to snatch a son from death's pilfering hand and return him to the arms of his mother.

The young man sits up and talks. What he says we are not told. But surely one of the first words to stumble from his lips is "Mother."

The miracle is an incredible display of the Savior's power. But there is something even more incredible about this auspicious meeting at the town gate.

This mother had not asked for a miracle. She had not thrown herself at the Savior's feet and begged for the life of her son. She hadn't demonstrated great faith. In fact, she hadn't demonstrated *any* faith at all. As far as we know, she didn't even know who Jesus was.

That is what's so incredible.

It is a miracle done without human prompting. Without thought of lessons to be taught to the disciples. Without thought of deity to be demonstrated to the skeptics.

It is a miracle drawn solely from the well of divine compassion. So free the water. So pure the heart from which it is drawn. So tender the hand that cups it and brings it to this bereaved mother's lips.

# PRAYER

ear Lord,

Thank you for how deep the well of your compassion is . . . and how pure . . . and how sweet. Thank you for how freely and spontaneously that water is given.

Thank you that it is not great knowledge or great wealth or great power that moves you to draw from that well, but something as small and weak and tender as tears.

Thank you, O most merciful Savior, for that spring day when you gave back that son to his mother. What a beautiful picture of compassion. And what an enticing picture of the spring yet to come, when you will wipe every tear from our eyes and when there will no longer be any sickness or death.

Give me the heart you had for that bereaved mother, for those whose shoulders are stooped low under the weight of a loss too great for them to bear.

I pray for those who have lost a loved one, whether by sudden accident or by a slow, agonizing disease.

> Grant them grace to bear the painful intro-spection of unanswered prayers.
> Grant them grace to know that though their prayers went unanswered, their *tears* did not go unnoticed.
> Grant them grace to know that he who no-tices when a sparrow falls to the ground, took note of their loss with *his* tears.

Especially I would like to pray for _____, whose heart is broken with grief . . .

# AN
## INCREDIBLE MOMENT
### IN A
### STORM

# SCRIPTURE

hat day when evening came, he said to his disciples, "Let us go over to the other side." Leaving the crowd behind, they took him along, just as he was, in the boat. There were also other boats with him. A furious squall came up, and the waves broke over the boat, so that it was nearly swamped. Jesus was in the stern, sleeping on a cushion. The disciples woke him and said to him, "Teacher, don't you care if we drown?"

He got up, rebuked the wind and said to the waves, "Quiet! Be still!" Then the wind died down and it was completely calm.

He said to his disciples, "Why are you so afraid? Do you still have no faith?"

They were terrified and asked each other, "Who is this? Even the wind and the waves obey him!"

*Mark 4:35–41*

# MEDITATION

or Jesus the days have been running together like one long, flowing, seamless garment that was fast beginning to smother him in its folds.

By day, he has revealed mysteries about the kingdom to the teeming masses. By the crackling light of the evening campfire, he has explained those mysteries to his closest circle of confidants. From the first pastels of dawn until the dying embers of midnight, Jesus has been tirelessly about his Father's business. Teaching. Healing the sick. Casting out demons. Performing miracles.

But now he is tired.

The constant crush of the crowds has given him no margin in which to rest or refresh himself. So when evening comes after another exhausting day of teaching, Jesus is ready for a sequestered Sabbath from the long week his body and soul have put in.

"Let's go over to the other side."

With the crowds growing smaller to dot the shore behind them, Jesus finds a cushion and cuddles up in the cupped, wooden hands of the stern. There, rocked by the idle rhythm of the lapping waves and fanned by the gentle hand of the demure wind, Jesus falls asleep.

The constellations, pricking through the black velvet of the sky, serve as a guide as the bow cuts a swath through the coarser fabric of the sea. The disciples are tired, too, but somehow the sea breeze and the proud sail fill their spirits enough to lift the heaviness from their eyes.

Suddenly, in a bracing affront to the calm idyllic night,

a gust of cold wind slaps the sail. The disciples are flounced to the hull where they find themselves caught up in the sweeping rage of a tempest. As they steady themselves in the canting vessel, a glinting blade of lightning rips through the sky.

Tirades of wind shriek at the sail, causing it to flap and pop in nervous response. In its fury the wind takes pitchforks from the sea and hurls them at the cowering disciples.

Heaving waves toss the boat back and forth on its frothy crests. Wave after wave bursts against its sides, each one sloshing more water into the boat. Some of the disciples frantically bail, while others pull at the oars, while still others wrestle to subdue the erratic sail.

Meanwhile, there is a calm eye in the midst of this storm. Jesus is fast asleep. What a profound slumber must have come over the wearied Messiah. And what a profound faith he must have in his Father's care. For it is not the wooden hands of the stern that shelter him from the storm, but the powerful hands of his heavenly Father.

Jesus, however, is the only one in the boat who knows that. The others are in a frenzy. With the sea threatening to swallow them, they shake Jesus awake, yelling at him to drown out the competing howls of the wind.

"Teacher, don't you care if we drown?"

Jesus awakes to a dozen pairs of faithless eyes, bloodshot with terror. He turns his piercing gaze toward the storm. He gets up and speaks to the wind first and then

☩

to the waves, almost as if speaking to unruly children, playing too loudly in the house.

"Quiet! Be still!"

Immediately the roughhousing stops. Without so much as a word or a whine or a whimper in reply.

The sail falls limp. The boat steadies itself. The storm is over.

The Lord then turns to rebuke his other children. "Why are you so afraid? Do you still have no faith?"

The disciples have seen Jesus give strength to lame legs, sight to blind eyes, and health to a centurion's servant. But they have never seen him do anything like this. It is the greatest unleashing of raw power they have ever witnessed.

But with the storm calmed and the danger of drowning behind them, why are they still afraid?

Why? Because within their minds they find themselves facing a more terrifying storm—a storm that came upon them as suddenly and as turbulently as the one they just survived. The vortex of that storm swirls around their master's identity.

"Who is this? Even the wind and the waves obey him!"

Then their eyes see.

He who stands before them is no mere teacher or prophet or faith healer. He who stands before them holds the wild mane of nature in the tight grip of his hands. To him, the unbridled forces of nature submit, without so much as a kick or a whinny of resistance.

And in the wet, shivering presence of such a power, the disciples stand terrified, knowing that the man who slept in the stern rose from that sleep to do what only God himself could do.

# PRAYER

ear Master of the Wind
and Waves,

Help me when the sudden storms of life come crashing over me with their fierce winds and frothing waves. I have seen enough storms, Lord, to know how quickly peaceful circumstances can turn into catastrophe.

I have seen the strong become weak with disease. I have seen the freest of spirits become enslaved with addiction. I have seen the brightest of stars fall like meteors in a streak of dying fame.

I have seen respected preachers and politicians disgraced to become the laughingstocks of the land.

I have seen banks go bankrupt, their riches taking wings on the updrafts of plummeting markets. I have seen fortunes lost in gold, silver, and precious stones. I have seen dynasties of oil, real estate, and stocks swept overboard to the bottom of the sea.

I have seen the faithful lose faith. I have seen happy marriages with hopeful beginnings end up on the rocks of infidelity. And I have seen prodigals blown off course to to sink in a sea of sin.

Yes, Lord, I have seen a lot of storms. Too many of other people's to feel untouchable. Too many of my own to feel critical or proud or unsympathetic.

Some dear people I love, Lord, are going through some tempestuous times right now. I pray that you would be with _____ and with _____ and with _____. Help them to see you in the midst of their storms—you who rule the wind and waves with only a word.

And help them to see that no matter how devastating the storm that sweeps over them, you *do* care if they drown. Help them not to be hasty in judging your concern for them during those times when their lives seem to be sinking and you seem to be asleep in the stern.

Help them to see that you allow storms in their lives to strengthen them—not to shipwreck them. And help them to see that it is you who not only point out the direction their lives should take but who ride with them to hasten their safe passage.

Thank you, Lord Jesus, for being there during their individual storms. And when uncertain seas unsettle their faith, turn their attention to you so that the tempest in their souls might be quieted and made still. . . .

# An
# INCREDIBLE MOMENT
# WITH THE
# FIVE THOUSAND

# Scripture

ome time after this, Jesus crossed to the far shore of the Sea of Galilee (that is, the Sea of Tiberias), and a great crowd of people followed him because they saw the miraculous signs he had performed on the sick. Then Jesus went up on a mountainside and sat down with his disciples. The Jewish Passover Feast was near.

When Jesus looked up and saw a great crowd coming toward him, he said to Philip, "Where shall we buy bread for these people to eat?" He asked this only to test him, for he already had in mind what he was going to do.

Philip answered him, "Eight months' wages would not buy enough bread for each one to have a bite!"

Another of his disciples, Andrew, Simon Peter's brother, spoke up, "Here is a boy with five small barley loaves and two small fish, but how far will they go among so many?"

Jesus said, "Have the people sit down." There was plenty of grass in that place, and the men sat down, about five thousand of them. Jesus then took the loaves, gave thanks, and distributed to those who were seated as much as they wanted. He did the same with the fish.

When they had all had enough to eat, he said to his disciples, "Gather the pieces that are left over. Let nothing be wasted."

So they gathered them and filled twelve baskets with the pieces of the five barley loaves left over by those who had eaten.

After the people saw the miraculous sign that Jesus did, they began to say, "Surely this is the Prophet who is to come into the world." Jesus, knowing that they in-tended to come and make him king by force, withdrew again to a mountain by himself. . . .

When they found him on the other side of the lake, they asked him, "Rabbi, when did you get here?"

Jesus answered, "I tell you the truth, you are looking for me, not because you saw miraculous signs but because you ate the loaves and had your fill. Do not work for food that spoils, but for food that endures to eternal life, which the Son of Man will give you. On him God the Father has placed his seal of approval."

Then they asked him, "What must we do to do the works God requires?"

Jesus answered, "The work of God is this: to believe in the one he has sent."

So they asked him, "What miraculous sign then will you give that we may see it and believe you? What will you do? Our forefathers ate the manna in the desert; as it is written: 'He gave them bread from heaven to eat.'"

Jesus said to them, "I tell you the truth, it is not Moses who has given you the bread from heaven, but it is my Father who gives you the true bread from heaven. For the bread of God is he who comes down from heaven and gives life to the world."

"Sir," they said, "from now on give us this bread."

Then Jesus declared, "I am the bread of life. He who comes to me will never go hungry. . . . "

*John 6:1–15, 25–35a*

✽

# MEDITATION

iracles are the common currency of heaven. The feeding of the five thousand was just a little loose change spilling from a hole in its pocket.

It is the only miracle recorded by all four Gospels. Of the four, only John gives the interpretation.

All day long Jesus has given himself to the crowd, one by one unloading the burdens from their tired backs. It is late in the day now, and the Savior is hungry and bone-weary from the endless press of the crowd. He tries to get a little rest by slipping away up the hillside with his disciples, but the crowd grants him no reprieve.

Nevertheless, Mark tells us that Jesus felt compassion on the people. They seemed to him like sheep without a shepherd. Without someone to lead them into the serene landscape of faith with its green pastures and still waters. Without someone to restore their souls. Without someone to guide them down the right paths or walk with them through life's dark valleys.

The disciples suggest that Jesus send the people away so they can go to the villages and find food. But Jesus is too good of a shepherd to do that.

When he sees the flock making its way up the hill, foraging for a few tender mercies, Jesus seizes the moment to test Philip's faith. "Where shall we buy bread for these people to eat?"

The disciple puts a sharp pencil to the problem and is quick to calculate the cost. He concludes that the expenditure is beyond their budget. He puts his pencil down. "Impossible. Can't be done."

We all have our own list of impossibilities: You can't make a silk purse out of a sow's ear . . . You can't get blood from a turnip . . . You can't change a leopard's spots.

Impossibilities? Not to the Word who was in the beginning *with* God, flinging galaxies into orbit. Not to the Word who *was* God, coming down from heaven to become flesh and dwell among us.

For Jesus knit the leadership of his church out of the coarse threads of fishermen and tax collectors . . . he got wine from ordinary tap water . . . and he changed a man, covered with leprous spots, and made him clean.

Andrew goes to a little more trouble to search for a solution. He doesn't look at what *can't* be done but at the little that *can* be done. In doing so, he finds a poor boy with five flat loaves of coarsely ground barley bread and a couple of fish in a wicker basket. "But how far will they go among so many?"

What Philip and Andrew don't see is that impossible situations are not solved by how much we have in our purses or in our baskets. Not by how adequate our bank account or how abundant our assets.

Impossibilities are solved by miracles—pennies from heaven. And Jesus had a pocketful. *That* is where the disciples were to go to get bread.

Jesus turns to the boy. He doesn't have much. And what he has isn't the best. It's the food of the poor: bread made from barley, not wheat; salted-down sardines, not lambchops.

But what he has is enough. For the surrender of a child and the compassion of a Savior are all that's needed for this miracle.

It is an incredible moment, and plans to make Jesus king spread through the crowd. But just as the Savior refused the crown offered to him by Satan in the wilderness, so he refuses the one offered now.

For Jesus knows that the way to the throne is not over the red carpet of his temptor or on the shoulders of his supporters. The way to the throne is the path charted by his father, up the stony path that led to Calvary.

It would be there that the bread of life would be broken . . . so that a world hungering for forgiveness could take and eat.

# PRAYER

ear Bread of Life,

I confess that sometimes I feel so inadequate to meet the crowd of needs that surrounds me. Like that little boy with the lunch basket, I feel that the loaves I have are so small and the fish, so few. How far will they go among so many?

And yet I know that you manifest power through the weak things of this world.

You used a barren couple past the age of childbearing to create a nation as populous as the sand on the seashore. You used a young shepherd with a slingshot to slay a giant. You used a poor little boy with five flat loaves of coarsely-ground barley bread and a couple of small fish to feed thousands.

Help me to see, Lord, that this is how you characteristically work.

Help me to see that I don't need the adequate bank account Philip recommended or the abundant assets Andrew hinted at. All I need is to place what I have in your hands, like that little boy did.

Give me the faith to realize that you will bless what I give, no matter how small the loaves or how few the fish. No matter how meager the time or the talents or the treasures I place in your hands, you will multiply them.

I don't have much, Lord, but I give you what I have. Take my coarsely-ground life and the small skills that accompany it. Take them into your hands, Lord. Bless them. Multiply them. Use them for your glory and for the good of others.

Help me to realize that you are the true bread of life. Whenever pangs of hunger grab at my soul, help me to see that the bread in other windows—no matter how seductive to the eye or sweet to the taste—is not what I should be eating. Train my spiritual palate to long for you. And teach me that you are my daily bread and all the bread I will ever need.

Lord Jesus, I have a friend who has never tasted such bread. Her name is _____. She has sampled from life's smorgasbord, tasted from all that life has to offer. But she is starved for something more. Starved for love. For acceptance. For forgiveness. For meaning and purpose.

Help me to lead her to you, Jesus. Prepare her heart. And prepare mine. Give me an extra measure of humility so that I might be, as someone once said, merely one beggar telling another beggar where to find bread. . . .

# AN
# INCREDIBLE MOMENT
# ON THE
# WATER

❦

# Scripture

mmediately Jesus made the disciples get into the boat and go on ahead of him to the other side, while he dismissed the crowd. After he had dismissed them, he went up on a mountainside by himself to pray. When evening came, he was there alone, but the boat was already a considerable distance from land, buffeted by the waves because the wind was against it.

During the fourth watch of the night Jesus went out to them, walking on the lake. When the disciples saw him walking on the lake, they were terrified. "It's a ghost," they said, and cried out in fear.

But Jesus immediately said to them: "Take courage! It is I. Don't be afraid."

"Lord, if it's you," Peter replied, "tell me to come to you on the water."

"Come," he said.

Then Peter got down out of the boat, walked on the water and came toward Jesus. But when he saw the wind, he was afraid and, beginning to sink, cried out, "Lord, save me!"

Immediately Jesus reached out his hand and caught him. "You of little faith," he said, "why did you doubt?"

And when they climbed into the boat, the wind died down. Then those who were in the boat worshiped him, saying, "Truly you are the Son of God."

*Matthew 14: 22–33*

# MEDITATION

ith the sea of hungry people miraculously fed, it would seem that the climate of popularity surrounding Jesus would smooth any waves of opposition.

But Jesus senses a change in the weather. Behind him is the chilly reminder that his forerunner has been beheaded. Before him is an ominous gathering of Pharisees and Sadducees on the horizon. There these disparate groups will bunch together in billows of antagonism to confront Jesus, testing him to produce some authenticating sign from heaven.

On that lonely hilltop, Jesus braces himself to face that storm. That's why he sends the disciples to the other side of the sea. He needs time by himself. To mourn. To pray. To ask for strength to face the torrential gale that is gathering force against him.

As he prays on that windswept hill, the disciples oar their way across the shivering bronze of the late afternoon sea.

With the sun westering away in a streak of saffron, the squall grows colder and more severe. And the oars grow ever heavier. Up, over, dip, puuulll. Up, over, dip, puuulll. For ten futile hours they row, all the while moving only a discouraging three-and-a-half-miles.

In spite of the knives of pain in their backs, the cramps in their forearms, and the blood on their hands, they are merely rowing in place, barely holding their ground.

Now it is a couple of hours before dawn. Spears of lightning impale themselves on the mountains, flashing silhouetted peaks against the night sky. And the timpani of thunder rolls dramatically in the ensuing darkness.

Writhing bodies of water heave their bulks to batter the boat's hull. Ragged waves fray into the night and lash their contempt on the backs of the beleaguered crew. The sting from pellets of water blurs their vision, but in the intermittent flashes of light they see a form making its way over the convulsing sea.

Are they beginning to hallucinate from fatigue? They ease off on the oars and rub their eyes. Is it a ghost, some spirit sent to harbinger their death? Or maybe to hasten it?

All their superstitions about the sea come rushing back to them, and they scream out in terror. Their cries mingle with the moan of the wind when suddenly the ghost speaks.

"Take courage. It is I. Don't be afraid."

They rub their eyes again and squint into the erratic darkness. They can't believe what they see.

Jesus.

And he's walking toward them. The closer he comes, the faster Peter's heart pounds. Suddenly, the tide of emotion changes from fear to longing.

"Lord, if it's you, tell me to come to you on the water."

Jesus extends the invitation to Peter's outstretched faith, "Come."

With his eyes transfixed on the Savior's, Peter vaults over the port side. And to the breathless amazement of the others, the water holds him up, holds him up on a sea that is still wild with rage.

Incredible.

They have seen Jesus do many unbelievable things, but now, now they see an ordinary man doing the miraculous, mirroring what they thought only Jesus could do.

But a windblown slap from the jealous sea turns Peter's head and brings him to his knees. In desperation he shouts.

"Lord, save me!"

And in that moment of faith, however sinking, he does. Jesus grips Peter's forearm and pulls him to safety.

Once Jesus boards the boat, the storm subsides. The lesson is over.

And what did the disciples learn?

Through Peter they gained a visual definition of faith, for what more is faith than stepping out in obedience to Jesus and looking to him to sustain our steps, even when the path of obedience takes us over uncertain and untamed waters.

Through Peter they also learned the difference between walking by faith and walking by sight. When the disciple fixed his eyes on the Savior, he walked on water. When he turned his eyes to the wind, he sank.

Undoubtedly, this storm on the Sea of Galilee loomed vivid in the disciples' minds as they would face the spiritual storm of mounting opposition. Like the actual storm, their encounter with the Pharisees and Sadducees was equally sudden, equally threatening, equally demanding in faith to keep their heads above water.

Just as quickly as the winds changed on the sea, so the crowds turned inclemently against Jesus: the one day wanting to crown him king, the other day wanting to crucify him. But because of the lessons they learned that night, the disciples would be prepared for this sudden gust of resistance.

When the controversy stormed about Jesus' identity, he asked Peter, "But what about you? Who do you say I am?" And Peter was able to turn his face from the caprice of the crowd, look Jesus straight in the eye, and say with steadfast faith, "You are the Christ, the Son of the living God."

Oh yes, the disciples learned one other thing.

Maybe it was years later after Jesus left them to ascend to the Father. Maybe it was in a quiet moment in the Upper Room, as they remembered him. Maybe it was in a moment of contemplation around a campfire on that Galilean seashore, as they stared up at the night sky and felt a sudden gust of chilly wind. Regardless of *when*, here is *what* they learned.

The disciples experienced two physical storms in their three-and-a-half-year residency with the Savior. In the first storm Jesus was present, only asleep. But in the next one he withdrew to a distant hill. And although he could see them, a blindfold of night prevented them from seeing him.

Why the withdrawal? To wean the disciples from sight to faith. To force them to rely less on their physical eyes and more on their spiritual ones.

If they were ever to walk by faith, Jesus had to withdraw from their sight.

Jesus couldn't have the disciples clinging to him as a trellis of support for the frail tendrils of their faith. Their roots must deepen. Their trunks must grow stout. Their branches must grow firm.

Otherwise, they would not be strong enough to stand alone, which they one day must do. Otherwise, they would not be able to support the fruit to be borne on their branches, which he was preparing them to bear in abundance.

It was a hard chapter in the textbook of faith. Within hours, their clothes would dry, their shivering would stop. Within days, they would forget their sore backs, forget their raw hands. But the lessons the disciples learned that night they would never forget.

# PRAYER

ear Lord Jesus,

Help me to learn the lessons of faith when life is calm so I may be prepared when the winds of adversity rise up against me.

Help me to understand, as I cling to the security of the seashore, that the hard lessons of faith are only learned on the open sea. Where the waves are rough. Where the wind is relentless. Where the risks are real.

There when I feel the sting of the wind in my face and the fury of the waves in my soul, may I learn to put my trust in you, not in the strength of my hands or in the smoothness of the circumstances that surround me.

Dearest Jesus, though you may be out of my sight during a storm, I thank you that I am never out of yours.

I pray now that you would turn your ever-watching, ever-caring eyes upon a couple I deeply care for. They are going through some stormy weather, and if you don't intervene, their marriage will certainly end up on the rocks.

I pray for _____ and _____. They desperately need you to come near, Lord. They are straining at their oars, struggling to be faithful to the course you've charted for their lives.

But their spirits are drenched with discouragement. Their backs are sore from the pull of responsibilities that fill their hands. Their minds shiver with the fear that this time they might not make it through the storm.

Have mercy on them, Jesus. They are weathered and

worn and want so much to find a peaceful harbor where they can find rest for their weary hearts.

Come to them. Let them see you in the midst of their storm. Let them hear your voice above the circumstances raging around them. Grant them the grace to fix their eyes on you, Lord, and not on the sting of circumstances whipping around them.

Help them to realize that even in their sinking moments, when life is heavy and their faith has lost its buoyancy, that you are there with an outstretched hand to keep them from going under. Calm their troubled hearts, Lord Jesus, and still this storm that so threatens their marriage. . . .

# AN
## INCREDIBLE MOMENT
## WITH A
## DEMONIZED BOY

# SCRIPTURE

he next day, when they came down from the mountain, a large crowd met him. A man in the crowd called out, "Teacher, I beg you to look at my son, for he is my only child. A spirit seizes him and he suddenly screams; it throws him into convulsions so that he foams at the mouth. It scarcely ever leaves him and is destroying him. I begged your disciples to drive it out, but they could not."

"O unbelieving and perverse generation," Jesus replied, "how long shall I stay with you and put up with you? Bring your son here."

Even while the boy was coming, the demon threw him to the ground in a convulsion. But Jesus rebuked the evil spirit, healed the boy and gave him back to his father. And they were all amazed at the greatness of God.

*Luke 9:37–43a*

# MEDITATION

he boy lies sleeping, curled in his covers and bronzed in the dying light of a small oil lamp. The father runs his hand over the boy's head, gently stroking his hair into place.

As he does, a solitary tear slides down his face.

A tear for the trade the boy will never learn, for the wife he will never love, for the children he will never look at as they lie sleeping in their beds.

Satan has robbed his son of all these.

The father's role as a parent has been reduced to that of a caretaker. He, too, has been robbed.

Robbed of the simple joys of parenthood. Robbed of all the hopes and dreams and aspirations that a father has for his son. Robbed of all the little-boy noises, of all the childish questions, of all the playful laughter, of all the father-to-son talks.

Anxious questions staunch that lone, mute tear: *What will happen when his mother and I die? Who will take him then? Who will feed him and look after him?*

His heart sinks for he knows the answer to all these questions: *No one.* No one wants a deaf mute prone to violent seizures.

The boy looks so peaceful, all snug in his bed. But his life is anything but that.

The seizures that come upon him are sporadic and sudden. And when they attack, he is thrown into a frothing fit, grinding his teeth and foaming at the mouth like a rabid animal.

When the seizure abates, the boy finds himself encircled by worried eyes. As he gets up, the people back away and scold him for being out on the streets.

Understandably, he is a child who is always off to himself, a lonely island of introspection surrounded by silence and by the stand-offish stares of those on the mainland.

The neighborhood kids are warned to stay away from him. Another robbery. Stolen are his playmates along with his childhood.

His life has been picked clean of anything of value, and he stands looking like some decrepit building—vacant, vandalized, and slated for demolition.

Around every corner lurks the potential for destruction. A cruel spirit lies in wait for him like a bully waiting to pounce on a kid coming home from school. It sneaks up on the boy, jumps him from behind, and mashes his face into the dirt—all the while, delighting in the tyranny.

This is our adversary, the Devil. This is who he is. In all his cowardice and cruelty. This is his way—to push, to shove, to brutalize.

Like a ravenous lion the devil roams about, seeking whom he may devour. Seeking someone he can get his paws on, sink his teeth into. Preying on the weak, the innocent, the defenseless. Savagely. Viciously. And as a lion cunningly stalks a group of antelopes, he singles out the youngest, most vulnerable one, and ruthlessly runs him down.

When the father hears that Jesus is in town, he turns

to him in hopes that the Redeemer can somehow bring his son back from the clutches of Satan's paws. He falls on his knees and clasps his hands in a desperate plea. He begs as only a parent in pain can.

Jesus sees his desperation and asks, "How long has he been like this?"

"From childhood. It has often thrown him into fire or water to kill him. But if you can do anything, take pity on us and help us."

" 'If you can'?" replies Jesus. "Everything is possible for him who believes."

With tears streaking his forlorn face, the father looks into Jesus' eyes and appeals to him, "I do believe; help me overcome my unbelief."

Jesus turns to the boy and addresses the demon within. "You deaf and mute spirit, I command you, come out of him and never enter him again."

The spirit shrieks, violently kicking the boy in a final, recalcitrant act before it leaves. The boy lies on the ground, limp and lifeless. The crowd murmurs, "He's dead." But Jesus grasps the boy's hand and pulls him to his feet.

The crowd breathes a collective sigh of relief at the incredible uprooting of evil that had so tenaciously wrapped itself around the boy's life.

Jesus hands the boy over to the emotional embrace of his father. Thus the Redeemer returns the stolen goods to their rightful owners. To a tearful father he gives back his son. And to the son, he gives back his childhood.

❦

# PRAYER

ear Lord,

As I see how insidious the enemy is, how ruthless, how unscrupulous, how cowardly, I despise him more than ever.

When I hear of children abused or kidnapped or killed, my emotions swing from a sunken feeling of remorse to sudden outrage. That's when my mind becomes crowded with questions: How could you allow the Devil so long a leash that he could devour defenseless children without restraint? Where were the angels that were supposed to guard them? Where were you when they cried for help?

Forgive me, but these are the questions I have when I lay the promises in my Bible next to the headlines in the newspaper.

Help me to understand. And where I can't understand, help me to trust. And where I can't trust, help me to overcome my unbelief.

O Good Shepherd, watch over all the little children. They are so helpless, and the night is so dark and so full of danger.

Especially I pray for those children who have been robbed physically . . .

> for the diabetic and epileptic, who live at the mercy of embarrassing and sometimes life-threatening seizures.
> for the deaf, who live so alone in a world of silence.
> for the mute, who ache to express themselves clearly.

Have mercy on them, Lord. They have special needs. And have mercy on their parents. They have special needs, too.

> Give them an extra measure of grace to meet the extraordinary demands of caring for their children.
>
> Give them strength for the uphill road they must travel.
>
> Give them tolerance for the insensitive, who stare and whisper.
>
> Give them freedom from feeling that they are being punished for something they did in the past.
>
> Give them release from the guilt that they are not doing enough for their child.
>
> Give them rest—both spiritually and physically. Heaven only knows how much they need it.

Thank you that you came expressly for the purpose of destroying the works of the Devil, to repair the damage he has done, to return what he has robbed.

Especially I pray that you would come to the aid of a child named _____, whose childhood is being stolen away. . . .

# AN
## INCREDIBLE MOMENT
## WITH A
## BENT-OVER WOMAN

# SCRIPTURE

n a Sabbath Jesus was teaching in one of the synagogues, and a woman was there who had been crippled by a spirit for eighteen years. She was bent over and could not straighten up at all. When Jesus saw her, he called her forward and said to her, "Woman, you are set free from your infirmity." Then he put his hands on her, and immediately she straightened up and praised God.

Indignant because Jesus had healed on the Sabbath, the synagogue ruler said to the people, "There are six days for work. So come and be healed on those days, not on the Sabbath."

The Lord answered him, "You hypocrites! Doesn't each of you on the Sabbath untie his ox or donkey from the stall and lead it out to give it water? Then should not this woman, a daughter of Abraham, whom Satan has kept bound for eighteen long years, be set free on the Sabbath day from what bound her?"

When he said this, all his opponents were humiliated, but the people were delighted with all the wonderful things he was doing.

*Luke 13:10–17*

# MEDITATION

he base of her back is fixed at a right angle, like a rusted hinge. Her back muscles are knotted to help bear the weight of the severe curvature, and her nerves are pinched from the misaligned vertebrae.

For almost two decades she has been tethered to this deformity, cinched tight by an emissary of Satan. A spirit has done a devilish dance on her back, leaving behind its cruel heel marks in trampling down what once stood tall and stately.

Above the bent woman arches an expansive sky where broken ranks of clouds parade by. But *her* movement is not so windblown and free. She winces in pain as she shuffles toward the synagogue.

She can't see the baby blue sky or the brilliant white billows overhead. She sees only the dirt brown streets and the litter of the day.

As she takes her seat in the synagogue, Jesus' attention is diverted from his text to fall upon the yellowed, dog-eared pages of her life. He skims the story of the last eighteen years, reading every sentence of suffering and pausing over every question mark that punctuates her pain. But what arrests his attention is the gilded edge on those pages—her faith.

She is a true daughter of Abraham. And she has come to worship Abraham's God, as she does every Sabbath. In spite of the pain. In spite of the pitied stares from adults. In spite of the giggled whispers from children at play in the streets.

Jesus closes the scroll he's been teaching from and bids

her to come to the front of the synagogue. It is an embarrassing moment for the woman. All eyes are riveted to her angular body as she makes her way awkwardly down the aisle.

She stops before him, twisting her torso in a strained attempt to see his face, and their eyes meet.

"Woman, you are freed from your sickness."

Jesus lays his hands on her hunched-over shoulders. And immediately the fisted muscles release their grip, the vertebrae fall into place, and the captive nerves are set free.

Like a cat arising from too long a nap, she stretches herself erect. As she does, eighteen years of misery tumble from her back to fall at the Savior's feet.

She raises her hands and turns her eyes toward heaven —something she hasn't been able to do for a long, long time—and praises the God of Abraham and Isaac and Jacob, praises him for also being the God of lonely, little, bent-over women.

But what glorifies God only infuriates the synagogue official. To him, the service has been disrupted and the Sabbath, dishonored. He rises in indignation to restore order and to make sure this breach of protocol doesn't set a precedent. His words have an edge on them and come down sharply on the crowd.

"There are six days for work. So come and be healed on those days, not on the Sabbath."

Wait a minute. Shouldn't he be rubbing his eyes rather than raising his voice? Did he somehow miss the miracle?

No, he saw it. But his eyes were so fixed on formality and rules and time-honored traditions that he lost sight of the incredible display of power right before his eyes.

Jesus turns to the pontifical man who is flanked by a few of the more pious.

"You hypocrites! Doesn't each of you on the Sabbath untie his ox or donkey from the stall and lead it out to give it water? Then should not this woman, a daughter of Abraham, whom Satan has kept bound for eighteen long years, be set free on the Sabbath day from what bound her?"

The logic proves irrefutable. All eyes turn to him. All ears await his reply. But the synagogue official sits down slowly in a stew of humiliating silence.

Such an ironic picture. The sudden flexibility of the woman's physical posture juxtaposed to the rigidity of the religious leader's spiritual posture.

Why is it that so often the most religious are the most resistant to the power of God? Is their theology so neatly boxed that there is no room for miracles? Is their order of service so structured that there is no room to be surprised by the spontaneity of a supernatural God?

*No room.*

Maybe that's the problem. Maybe that's why they close the door on the supernatural—there's no room in the inn of their hearts for the birth of something unexpected from heaven.

# PRAYER

ear Lord Jesus,

I pray for all who are in some way bent low, whether by an aberration of genetics or by accident or by an emissary of Satan. I pray for those who see ground instead of sky. For those whose eyes are filled with dirt and litter and the monotonous gray of concrete instead of with clouds and birds and rainbows.

I pray for those whose bodies are bent from osteoporosis or arthritis or scoliosis. For those imprisoned between the rails of hospital beds. For those confined to wheelchairs. For those who cannot move about without braces or crutches or walkers.

Remember the crippled who lean on you, Lord, clumsily making their way to church every Sunday, yet who do not receive the healing they so desperately pray for.

Remember the bedridden who stare all day long at the ceiling, straining to see you in the midst of all their suffering.

Remember those young whose bodies have stolen away their childhood, and those elderly whose bodies have refused to let them grow old gracefully.

Have mercy on them all, dear Jesus. Touch them. Lift the burden of their infirmities from their shoulders. And if it be your will that their conditions continue, give them stronger faith so they may bear their burdens, and stronger friends to bear what they cannot bear themselves.

For those whose souls are bent low to the ground under the weight of regret, relieve them of the guilt that keeps them from walking erect.

Loose them from the burdens of the past that are strapped so tightly to their backs—of decisions made in passion that still haunt them . . . of words spoken in anger that still echo in their minds . . . of things taken in selfishness that are to this day regretted.

Touch them, too, Lord. Lift the burdens of the past from their slumped-over souls.

Especially I pray for _____, who is bent over in body and for _____, who is bent over in soul. They are weary and heavy laden, Lord. Bid them to come to you. There may they lay down their burdens. And there may they find rest for their souls.

Grant them both the tender mercy of your healing touch. And grant that they may stand tall once again and see sky. . . .

# An
## INCREDIBLE MOMENT
## WITH
## LAZARUS

ow a man named Lazarus was sick. He was from Bethany, the village of Mary and her sister Martha. This Mary, whose brother Lazarus now lay sick, was the same one who poured perfume on the Lord and wiped his feet with her hair. So the sisters sent word to Jesus, "Lord, the one you love is sick."

When he heard this, Jesus said, "This sickness will not end in death. No, it is for God's glory so that God's Son may be glorified through it." Jesus loved Martha and her sister and Lazarus. Yet when he heard that Lazarus was sick, he stayed where he was two more days.

Then he said to his disciples, "Let us go back to Judea."

"But Rabbi," they said, "a short while ago the Jews tried to stone you, and yet you are going back there?"

Jesus answered, "Are there not twelve hours of daylight? A man who walks by day will not stumble, for he sees by this world's light. It is when he walks by night that he stumbles, for he has no light."

After he had said this, he went on to tell them, "Our friend Lazarus has fallen asleep; but I am going there to wake him up."

His disciples replied, "Lord, if he sleeps, he will get better." Jesus had been speaking of his death, but his disciples thought he meant natural sleep.

So then he told them plainly, "Lazarus is dead, and for your sake I am glad I was not there, so that you may believe. But let us go to him."

Then Thomas (called Didymus) said to the rest of the

disciples, "Let us also go, that we may die with him."

On his arrival, Jesus found that Lazarus had already been in the tomb for four days. Bethany was less than two miles from Jerusalem, and many Jews had come to Martha and Mary to comfort them in the loss of their brother. When Martha heard that Jesus was coming, she went out to meet him, but Mary stayed at home.

"Lord," Martha said to Jesus, "if you had been here, my brother would not have died. But I know that even now God will give you whatever you ask."

Jesus said to her, "Your brother will rise again."

Martha answered, "I know he will rise again in the resurrection at the last day."

Jesus said to her, "I am the resurrection and the life. He who believes in me will live, even though he dies; and whoever lives and believes in me will never die. Do you believe this?"

"Yes, Lord," she told him, "I believe that you are the Christ, the Son of God, who was to come into the world."

And after she had said this, she went back and called her sister Mary aside. "The Teacher is here," she said, "and is asking for you." When Mary heard this, she got up quickly and went to him. Now Jesus had not yet entered the village, but was still at the place where Martha had met him. When the Jews who had been with Mary in the house, comforting her, noticed how quickly she got up and went out, they followed her, supposing she was going to the tomb to mourn there.

When Mary reached the place where Jesus was and saw him, she fell at his feet and said, "Lord, if you had been here, my brother would not have died."

When Jesus saw her weeping, and the Jews who had come along with her also weeping, he was deeply moved in spirit and troubled. "Where have you laid him?" he asked.

"Come and see, Lord," they replied.

Jesus wept.

Then the Jews said, "See how he loved him!"

But some of them said, "Could not he who opened the eyes of the blind man have kept this man from dying?"

Jesus, once more deeply moved, came to the tomb. It was a cave with a stone laid across the entrance. "Take away the stone," he said.

"But, Lord," said Martha, the sister of the dead man, "by this time there is a bad odor, for he has been there four days."

Then Jesus said, "Did I not tell you that if you believed, you would see the glory of God?"

So they took away the stone. Then Jesus looked up, and said, "Father, I thank you that you have heard me. I knew that you always hear me, but I said this for the benefit of the people standing here, that they may believe that you sent me."

When he had said this, Jesus called in a loud voice, "Lazarus, come out!" The dead man came out, his hands and feet wrapped with strips of linen, and a cloth around his face.

Jesus said to them, "Take off the grave clothes and let him go."

*John 11: 1–44*

# MEDITATION

eath is the way of all flesh—a season to spring forth and flower, a season to fade and fall to the ground.

But if the seasons teach us anything, if they make one grand, eloquent statement at all, it is that death does not have the last word. True, the flower's petals fall to the ground. But so do its seeds. And though the seeds may sleep for a season under a blanket of snow, they will awake in spring.

As they do, they lift their fragrant heads to hint of a springtime yet to come. Where flowers never die. Where the dew of tears never falls.

But the elysian fields of paradise are far from the borders of Bethany. There, an untimely frost has settled over a friend. Lazarus is wilting fast. The news comes by way of a messenger.

"Lord, the one you love is sick."

Oddly, Jesus doesn't rush to his bedside. Not because he is too busy. Or because he doesn't care. But because the Father is orchestrating an incredible moment and needs time to set the stage. And since a corpse must be center stage before this drama can begin, Jesus must wait until Lazarus dies before he can make his entrance.

But Mary and Martha can't see backstage in heaven. All they can see is an expansive, black curtain drawn across their lives. They sit at home, despondent, as in an empty theater, their tearful prayers returning to them like hollow echoes off indifferent walls.

It has been four days since their brother has died, but a mountain of grief still looms before them. It is a steep climb for the two sisters, and they feel they will never get over it. As Jesus approaches the outskirts of the city, a disillusioned Martha rushes out to meet him.

"Lord, if you had been here, my brother would not have died."

Jesus meets her on the crumbling ledge of her grief. He steadies her with the assurance that he is in control.

"I am the resurrection and the life. He who believes in me will live, even though he dies."

The words provide a foothold for her. At Jesus' request, Martha goes to call her sister. Mary comes, her eyes puffy and bloodshot. The flood of emotions is still swift and turbid. She falls before the Lord like an earthenware vessel dropped to the ground, her heart shattered, her tears spilling over his feet.

"Lord, if you had been here, my brother would not have died."

Both sisters approached Jesus with the identical words. But whereas Martha said them to his face, Mary cried them at his feet. Maybe that is why the one evokes only a theological truth, while the other evokes his tears.

Twice the Scriptures blot the tears of our Lord. On a hill overlooking Jerusalem, as he weeps for the nation. And on the way to a friend's grave, as he weeps with those who grieve.

What an incredible Savior. Weeping not just *for* us in

our sin but *with* us in our suffering. Stooping to share our yoke so the burden of grief may be lessened.

But how do the tears he shared with Mary fit with the theological truth he shared with Martha? Who can reconcile the words "Jesus wept" with " 'I am the resurrection and the life' "?

So strange that one with such absolute power would surrender so quickly to so small an army as tears.

But he does.

And, for a beautifully tender moment, we are given the privilege to glimpse one of the most provocative embraces between deity and humanity in all the Scriptures.

On our way to Lazarus' tomb we stumble on still another question. Jesus approaches the gravesite with the full assurance that he will raise his friend from the dead. Why then does the sight of the tomb trouble him?

Maybe the tomb in the garden is too graphic a reminder of Eden gone to seed. Of Paradise lost. And of the cold, dark tomb he would have to enter to regain it.

In any case, it is remarkable that *our* plight could trouble *his* spirit; that *our* pain could summon *his* tears.

The raising of Lazarus is the most daring and dramatic of all the Savior's healings. He courageously went into a den where hostility raged against him to snatch a friend from the jaws of death.

It was an incredible moment.

It revealed that Jesus was who he said he was—the

resurrection and the life. But it revealed something else.

The tears of God.

And who's to say which is more incredible—a man who raises the dead . . . or a God who weeps?

# PRAYER

ear Lord Jesus,

Thank you for that shortest but sweetest verse in all the Bible—"Jesus wept." Thank you for those tears you cried so openly. They have given not only dignity to my grief but freedom to my emotions.

Thank you for the beautiful tribute that tears are to the dead, telling them they were loved and will be missed.

Help me realize that if the death of a loved one was difficult for you—*you*, the Resurrection and the Life— then I need never be ashamed when it is difficult for me.

Thank you that you know what it's like to lose someone you love. And for the assurance that when I come to you in my grief, you know how I feel.

Thank you that my tears can evoke yours.

Help me to follow the trail of tears you left behind on the way to Lazarus' tomb so that I may learn to weep with those who weep.

Help me to feel the pain they feel . . . the uncertainty . . . the fear . . . the heaviness . . . the regret . . . the despondency.

I pray for all who grieve the loss of a loved one,

> for the one who has lost a parent . . .
> for the one who has lost a child . . .
> for the one who has lost a grandparent . . .
> for the one who has lost a sister . . .
> for the one who has lost a brother . . .
> for the one who has lost a friend . . .

I pray for those who cry out with Martha and Mary, "Lord, if you had been there. . . ." In the emotional blur caused by their loss, help them to see that you *were* there, weeping with them.

Especially I pray for _____. . . .

# AN
# INCREDIBLE MOMENT
# WITH A
# BLIND MAN

# SCRIPTURE

s Jesus approached Jericho, a blind man was sitting by the roadside begging. When he heard the crowd going by, he asked what was happening. They told him, "Jesus of Nazareth is passing by."

He called out, "Jesus, Son of David, have mercy on me!"

Those who led the way rebuked him and told him to be quiet, but he shouted all the more, "Son of David, have mercy on me!"

Jesus stopped and ordered the man to be brought to him. When he came near, Jesus asked him, "What do you want me to do for you?"

"Lord, I want to see," he replied.

Jesus said to him, "Receive your sight; your faith has healed you." Immediately he received his sight and followed Jesus, praising God. When all the people saw it, they also praised God.

*Luke 18:35–43*

# MEDITATION

is name, Mark tells us, is Bartimaeus. He is a blind beggar. His little space beside the road is home. Trodden dirt is his bed; a stone, his pillow.

Like the litter that collects in the gutter, he sits there day in, day out, a crumpled-up man on the side of the road. His friends are the discards that life, in its hurry, has left behind. Used-up, thrown-away people. Living in their own separate place. Living in their own separate pain.

Each has a story to tell. But it's a story nobody wants to hear.

They cry out for a touch, a kind word, a snippet of conversation. They cry out, but the world passes by on the road to somewhere else.

Feeling around in the dark, Bartimaeus accosts a passer-by with his searching hands. "Alms. Alms for the poor. Pity on a blind man." And thus he gropes for his daily bread.

A mumbled blessing. A coin in the cup from a reluctant benefactor. A sharp point of theology thrust at him from one of the more religious. A brusque shove to the side of the road.

This is what life is like for Bartimaeus.

For him the road is a dark stream where currents of voices rush by. He hears trickles of conversation down the street. But as the people get closer, they wriggle past him and are gone. He feels around in this dark stream, hoping to grab one of those voices by the gills and land himself a little something to eat. But it's like chasing minnows, and most slip through his hands.

Living on the roadside, he takes what comes his way: a coin in the cup, a slap on the hand, a blessing, a curse. This day what comes his way is a babble of voices: "Jesus . . . the Nazarene . . . Jesus is passing by."

He knows that name. He has heard of this man Jesus. Many say he is the future king and heir to David's throne. They say he's the servant Isaiah prophesied about:

> A light to the Gentiles,
> To open eyes that are blind
> and release from the dungeon
> those who sit in darkness.

O the dungeon Bartimaeus has been in for so long, locked away and forgotten. O the darkness, the loneliness, the rub of the shackles.

There on the roadside he sits, solitary in his thoughts, like a rock around which the stream of people flows.

*I must find him,* he thinks. *I must talk to this Jesus.* And he shouts from the roadside, "Son of David, have mercy on me!"

The crowd raps a few brittle words against him to keep him in his place. But Bartimaeus only redoubles his efforts. The veins protrude on his neck as he shouts, "SON OF DAVID, HAVE MERCY ON ME!"

Jesus stops and sends for the man. Bartimaeus casts aside his cloak and jumps to his feet. Condescending whispers hush as the blind man approaches. He stands now before the heir not only to David's throne but to the throne of heaven. And for a moment in time this blind beggar has the undivided attention of Deity.

"What do you want me to do for you?"

Can you believe your ears? Incredible. A blind man standing before the magistrate of heaven, the one who gave light to the sun, the moon, and the stars. And the response is not one of an exalted king but of a lowly servant. "What do you want me to do for you?"

Without hesitation Bartimaeus answers, "Lord, I want to see."

I want out of the dungeon, out of the darkness. I want out of the shackles of these blind eyes. I want out of the prison. I want to be free. "I want to see."

I want to get off of the roadside. I want to walk the streets of Jericho without running into its walls. I want to look in the shops. I want to find my way to the synagogue. "I want to see."

I want to use my hands for something besides feeling my way in the dark. I want to make things. I want to fix my own meals. I want to read. "I want to see."

I want to look into the eyes of a friend. I want to wave at someone across the way. I want to smile at children and pat their heads and wish them well. I want to love. I want to laugh. I want to live. "I want to see."

In an instant Jesus knows everything those four short words mean to this man. And the king shows him favor: "Receive your sight."

In the twinkling of an eye, Bartimaeus passes out of darkness and into the light.

Sunshine floods his eyes. He sees the azure sky . . . the armada of clouds in full sail . . . the pair of turtledoves winging their way just above the rooftops. He sees the buildings . . . the amazed faces of the crowd . . . and then he turns and sees Jesus. He sees the tenderness. He sees the love. He sees the eyes of a king.

His faith has healed him. Faith enough to make a fool of himself by shouting and stopping the crowd. Faith enough to come to Jesus. Faith enough to ask what no one but God could grant. Quite a lot to see, for a blind man.

And without looking back this new citizen of the kingdom joins that royal entourage down the Jericho road. To follow a king in whose eyes he has found favor. And to leave forever behind his beggar's space along that roadside.

# PRAYER

ear Son of David,

I pray you would give me a heart for those on the roadside. For those who, for whatever reason, are not in the mainstream of life. For those who lie crumpled and cast aside. For those who are forgotten and ignored. For those who are in some way blinded to the fullness of life.

Help me not to turn a deaf ear when they call out. Help me to stop, regardless of what the crowd may say. Help me to give them my undivided attention. Help me to give myself to them as you did—to show mercy, to do what I can.

And though I may not be able to loose them from their chains or free them from their separate prisons,

> help me to visit faithfully so they may know that someone cares;
> help me to bring a meal so they may be nourished;
> help me to say a kind word so they may be encouraged;
> help me to give a gentle touch so they may be comforted;
> help me to provide a blanket so they may be made warm;
> help me to give a pillow so they may have a soft place to lay their heads;
> help me to lend a listening ear so their stories may be heard.

Help me whenever, wherever, and however I can to bring light to someone who sits in darkness. And though

I may not be able to bring sight to their eyes, enable me to chase away a few shadows so their lives might be a little brighter.

Especially I pray for _____. . . .

# AN
# INCREDIBLE MOMENT
# IN AN
# OLIVE GROVE

# Scripture

hen he had finished praying, Jesus left with his disciples and crossed the Kidron Valley. On the other side there was an olive grove, and he and his disciples went into it.

Now Judas, who betrayed him, knew the place, because Jesus had often met there with his disciples. So Judas came to the grove, guiding a detachment of soldiers and some officials from the chief priests and Pharisees. They were carrying torches, lanterns and weapons.

Jesus, knowing all that was going to happen to him, went out and asked them, "Who is it you want?"

"Jesus of Nazareth," they replied.

"I am he," Jesus said. (And Judas the traitor was standing there with them.) When Jesus said, "I am he," they drew back and fell to the ground.

Again he asked them, "Who is it you want?"

And they said, "Jesus of Nazareth."

"I told you that I am he," Jesus answered. "If you are looking for me, then let these men go." This happened so that the words he had spoken would be fulfilled: "I have not lost one of those you gave me."

Then Simon Peter, who had a sword, drew it and struck the high priest's servant, cutting off his right ear. (The servant's name was Malchus.)

Jesus commanded Peter, "Put your sword away! Shall I not drink the cup the Father has given me?" . . .

And he touched the man's ear and healed him.

*John 18:1–11, Luke 22:51b*

# MEDITATION

esus emerges from the Garden of Gethsemane after his agonizing ordeal in prayer, sweaty from the struggle. But the heart that was poured out so emotionally is now filled with resolve to drink the cup set before him. No matter how bitter. No matter how difficult to swallow.

Jesus and his sleepy disciples descend into the Kidron Valley. Awaiting the Savior on the other side is a towering fate that casts a long, dark shadow over the valley. Coming up from the valley, Jesus enters an olive grove. He has come there often with his disciples.

This time would be his last.

In the grove the rheumatoid forms of the trees look as if they have grown out of some silent pain deep within the earth. They are old and have seen many injustices in their lives. Tonight they would witness the worst.

As he pauses in that shadowy respite, Jesus knows everything that is about to happen. He knows where he will be taken prisoner, when, and by whom. Yet he does nothing to postpone his appointment with destiny.

His hour has come.

Through the grove comes the muted clatter of what sounds like a mob. Torches bob above the crowd, curling plumes of black smoke into the night. As the disciples squint through the gnarled silhouettes of the trees, they discover that the mob is comprised of military men.

They are a detachment of soldiers from the peace-keeping force quartered in the tower of Antonia that overlooks the temple. The detachment numbers about six hundred men—a *tour de force* to ensure the arrest and crush any backlash of resistance.

How ironic. A detachment of soldiers coming for the One who could, with a whispered prayer, deploy legions of angels for his defense. How very ironic. Coming for the light of the world with torches and lanterns. Coming with hand-crafted swords and clubs for the one who forged the stars.

They come at night, strategically, to minimize the resistance. Since Jerusalem is brimming with pilgrims to celebrate Passover, there is no way of knowing how many of them are loyal to this brash young preacher. If the arrest were to take place during the day, it could make for an ugly scene, if not trigger a revolt.

The disciples dart their eyes over the grove to look for other soldiers, as well as for an avenue of escape. But before they realize it, the soldiers are upon them.

Peter's hand clutches the hilt of his recently purchased sword, but he makes no move to draw it. Wait. A sword? In the hands of a fisherman? What's gotten into Peter? Doesn't he realize that Jesus' kingdom is not of this world? Doesn't he know that his hands should be clasped in prayer, not around the hilt of a sword?

The flickering torchlight mottles the crowd, sending a circumference of shadows shivering on the ground.

Jesus steps forward. Courageously. Resolutely. An unarmed man squared off against a small army. He is the first to speak.

"Who is it you want?"

The reply is as crisp as the night air.

"Jesus the Nazarene."

Without hesitation or a ploy to cloak his identity, Jesus answers.

"I am he."

His confession is literally, "I am"—the same words God used to identify himself when speaking to Moses from the burning bush.

> "Moses said to God, 'Suppose I go to the Israelites and say to them, "The God of your fathers has sent me to you," and they ask me, "What is his name?" Then what shall I tell them?'
>
> "God said to Moses, 'I AM WHO I AM. This is what you are to say to the Israelites: "I AM has sent you."'"

Earlier in his ministry Jesus claimed equality with the Father when he said, "Before Abraham was born, *I am!* " At those words the religious leaders took up stones to kill him, for they understood his claim and denounced it as blasphemy.

At the words, "I am," the soldiers collapse. In one brief but incredible display of deity, Jesus overpowers his opposition.

They are thrust to the ground as a wrestler would pin down his opponent. But the force is exerted only momentarily. The display is not to defeat his enemy but merely to validate his claim.

Also, it is important to Jesus that he goes submissively, as a lamb led to slaughter, not as a cornered animal fighting for his life.

Again Jesus asks who they are looking for. Again they reply. Again he identifies himself. But this time he includes a plea for his disciples:

"If you are looking for me, then let these men go."

Judas then steps from the shadows to point out Jesus to his captors. And he does so, deceitfully, with a kiss.

"Friend," Jesus says to him, "do what you came for."

The words carry no hate—only sadness for a misguided friend on the path to his own destruction.

The servant of the high priest advances to take Jesus into custody. As he does, Peter whips out his sword and takes a swing at the man. The servant jerks his head out of the way, but the sword manages to sever part of his ear.

Jesus steps between the men and holds Peter at bay.

> "Put your sword back in its place, for all who
> draw the sword shall die by the sword. Do
> you think I cannot call on my Father, and
> he will at once put at my disposal more than
> twelve legions of angels? Shall I not drink
> the cup the Father has given me?"

Jesus turns his attention to the servant cupping his ear. He touches the wound. Immediately it is healed.

Jesus will not tolerate so much as the loss of an ear in his defense. He is insistent—the only blood shed would be his own.

The physician Luke describes the extent of the servant's wound. He uses the diminutive form of the word "ear" to indicate that only a small portion was actually cut off. Possibly something as small as the lobe.

Luke is also the only gospel writer to document the healing. Maybe to the others the miracle seemed minuscule in light of the tragedy being enacted before them. After all, of what consequence is the earlobe of a servant when the Savior of the world's life is at stake?

It was the last miracle Jesus performed before he died.

And the smallest.

Certainly the servant could have lived a full life without part of one of his ears. It wouldn't have impaired his hearing. At worst, the damage would have been cosmetic.

But he who preached "love your enemies" practiced what he preached—and practiced it to the end. For the Savior's last miracle was an unrequested act of kindness to an enemy.

Maybe it wasn't such a small miracle after all.

In light of the the legions of angels at his disposal and in light of how the Savior *could* have used his power, maybe, just maybe, it was his greatest.

# PRAYER

 earest Lord Jesus,

How courageously you faced the hour of your betrayal.
How you gave, even when you were being taken away to
death.

> To your father, you gave your obedience.
> To your disciples, you gave a plea for their
>     escape.
> To your betrayer, you gave a kind word.
> To your enemy, you gave healing.
> To your captors, you gave your own life.

Grant me the grace to confront life the way you did
in that olive grove on the night of your betrayal.

> When someone betrays me, grant me such a
>     forgiving heart that I would offer a kind
>     word in exchange for a deceitful kiss.
> When danger surrounds me, grant me such
>     faithfulness for my friends that I would
>     think of their welfare before my own.
> When an army of opposition mounts against
>     me, grant me the courage to stand alone.

Thank you, Lord, that something as small as a servant's
ear was not overlooked on your way to redeeming the
world. Thank you for all the lessons that small act of
kindness teaches.

I pray for the Malchuses in my life, those who have
aligned themselves with my opposition. Especially I pray
for anyone who has been hurt by a sharp word or deed
wielded by a friend in my defense.

Help me to show kindness to that person, even if it is a very small kindness. And in your powerful name I pray you would use that small kindness for that person's healing.

Thank you, Lord Jesus for all you have shown me of your glory, from the glory you revealed at a wedding in Cana to the glory you revealed in the Garden of Gethsemane. Open my eyes that I may see more. And open my heart that what I see may bring me to my knees to worship a truly incredible Savior. . . .

"Blessed are the eyes
that see what you see.
For I tell you that
many prophets and kings
wanted to see what you see
but did not see it. . . ."